I0202612

UNLOCKING THE POWER OF CONNECTION: MASTERING DIFFICULT CONVERSATIONS WITH CHALLENGING PERSONALITIES

ABSTRACT

An experiential learning experience on mastering difficult conversations. Learn essential skills to navigate challenges effectively, develop resilience, build rapport, and foster a positive work environment. Gain confidence in active listening, assertive communication, and conflict resolution to transform difficult interactions into opportunities for growth and stronger connections. Unlock the power of connection in challenging conversations.

Dr. Patrick C. Patrong
President/CEO Patrong Enterprises, Inc.

Unlocking the Power of Connection

Mastering Difficult Conversations
with Challenging Personalities

Dr. Patrick C. Patrong

President/CEO
Patrong Enterprises, Inc.

Richmond, VA

Unlocking the Power of Connection: Mastering Difficult Conversations with Challenging Personalities

For information regarding permissions or speaking engagements, contact:
Patrong Enterprises, Inc.

Richmond, Virginia   Telephone/WhatsApp: 1.410.294.5431
Website: www.patrongenterprises.com   Email: info@patrongenterprises.com

All examples, case studies, and scenarios in this book are inspired by real organizational settings but are presented in a composite form to preserve confidentiality and learning value. Names, roles, and details have been altered.

Printed in the United States of America.

ISBN: 979-8-9998411-1-7

Library of Congress Control Number: *Pending*

Design and Layout: Patrong Enterprises, Inc. **Cover Design:** "PEI Creative Studio 1A

First Edition: 2025

Legal Disclaimer
This publication is intended to provide general leadership and supervisory guidance. It is not intended to substitute for legal, human resources, or compliance advice tailored to any specific organization. Readers should consult their agency or legal counsel before applying any policies or procedures discussed in this book.

Preface

Conversations define relationships, and relationships define culture. Yet, the moments when communication matters most are often the hardest to navigate. *Unlocking the Power of Connection: Mastering Difficult Conversations with Challenging Personalities* was written for leaders, supervisors, and professionals who find themselves standing at the intersection of emotion, expectation, and accountability, those moments where silence feels safer than speaking, and tension quietly erodes trust.

This book was born out of decades spent in leadership, watching how unresolved issues can fracture teams and how courageous, well-handled dialogue can restore them. It offers more than techniques—it presents a mindset. Difficult conversations are not about winning an argument or managing a personality; they are about building understanding, promoting clarity, and sustaining respect even when comfort is impossible.

Throughout these pages, you will find practical strategies rooted in emotional intelligence, communication science, and leadership experience. You will learn how to manage your emotions under pressure, recognize defensive behavior, and approach conflict with empathy and precision. Most importantly, you will discover how to turn discomfort into opportunity—how to transform resistance into cooperation and confrontation into connection.

Whether you are a supervisor guiding a team, a manager addressing performance, or a leader shaping organizational culture, this work invites you to lead conversations that heal rather than harm. Every exchange becomes a chance to build trust, strengthen relationships, and model the kind of communication that drives excellence.

May this book serve as both a guide and a companion as you unlock the power of connection—one conversation at a time.

Table of Contents

Understanding Difficult Conversations..3

Exploring Impacts of Unresolved Issues 9

Identifying Personal Triggers and Emotional Intelligence......................17

Recognizing and Managing Defensive Behaviors....................................29

Effective Communication Techniques...37

Handling Conflict and Negotiating Win-Win Solutions.........................45

Strategies for Handling Passive-Aggressive Behaviors 53

Maintaining Emotional Resilience...61

Creating an Action Plan...69

Wrap-up and Conclusion...73

Understanding Difficult Conversations

Difficult conversations are inevitable in leadership, and understanding how to navigate them effectively is crucial for maintaining healthy relationships and fostering growth. This section will delve into the essence of difficult conversations and Challenging Personalities. By exploring the common challenges and barriers we encounter during these conversations, we will gain valuable insights into their impact on both personal and organizational levels. Understanding the underlying dynamics enables us to develop strategies that transform difficult conversations into meaningful dialogue and opportunities for resolution.

Defining Difficult Conversations and Challenging Personalities

Difficult conversations are an inevitable and challenging aspect of leadership. They arise when we need to address sensitive topics, confront conflicts, or deliver unwelcome feedback. Engaging in these conversations requires unique skills and strategies to navigate them effectively and achieve positive outcomes. Central to these difficult conversations are challenging personalities. These individuals present specific challenges due to their behaviors, attitudes, or communication styles. This section will explore the essence of difficult conversations and the people involved, highlighting their impact on leaders and organizations. By gaining a deeper understanding of these concepts, leaders can better prepare themselves to engage in productive and constructive dialogue, even in challenging circumstances.

Defining Difficult Conversations

Difficult conversations can be defined as exchanges that involve emotionally charged topics, opposing viewpoints, or high stakes, often resulting in tension, discomfort, or conflict. These conversations require courage, practical communication skills, and emotional intelligence to navigate successfully. Examples of difficult conversations include providing constructive criticism, addressing performance issues, discussing conflicts or grievances, negotiating delicate matters, or delivering challenging news. Such conversations can occur in various professional settings, from one-on-one interactions to team meetings or even across organizational hierarchies.

Difficult conversations are distinct from routine conversations due to their inherent complexity and potential for adverse consequences. They often involve managing intense emotions, defusing conflicts, and seeking mutually beneficial resolutions. The outcome of these conversations can have a significant impact on relationships, teamwork, employee morale, and the overall organizational culture. Therefore, it becomes imperative for leaders to be adept at recognizing, initiating, and managing difficult conversations with finesse and sensitivity.

Defining Challenging Personalities

Challenging personalities, on the other hand, possess certain traits, behaviors, or communication styles that make interactions with them particularly difficult. These individuals may exhibit a range of characteristics, including defensiveness, aggressiveness, passivity, resistance, or manipulative tendencies. Challenging Personalities can disrupt team dynamics, impede progress, create toxic work environments, and hinder communication.

It is crucial to note that the label "difficult person" does not imply that these individuals are inherently flawed or malicious. Instead, it suggests that their behaviors or interpersonal styles may hinder productive dialogue and lead to adverse outcomes. Challenging personalities may exhibit these challenging traits due to personal experiences, insecurities, misaligned expectations, or differing communication preferences. As leaders, it is essential to approach challenging personalities with empathy and strive to understand the underlying reasons for their challenging behavior.

_____

_____

_____

Effectively managing difficult conversations with challenging personalities requires a multifaceted approach. Leaders must develop various skills, including active listening, empathy, emotional regulation, assertive communication, and conflict resolution. By fostering an environment of psychological safety, leaders can encourage open dialogue, trust, and respect, even when addressing sensitive or contentious topics. Additionally, it is crucial to recognize the diversity of communication styles and adapt strategies to meet the individual needs of each person.

Difficult conversations and challenging personalities are intertwined aspects of leadership that demand attention and skillful navigation. Recognizing the complexities of these interactions enables leaders to approach them with preparedness, empathy, and a commitment to fostering positive outcomes. By understanding the essence of difficult conversations and the unique challenges presented by challenging personalities, leaders can embark on a journey of growth, building stronger relationships, promoting effective communication, and creating a culture of openness, collaboration, and success.

_____

_____

_____

Mental Shifts in Difficult Conversations

In challenging situations, navigating difficult conversations can be daunting. However, embracing four key shifts in mindset can transform how you approach these conversations, increasing your chances of achieving positive outcomes. These shifts involve reframing your perspective from focusing on individuals to understanding the situation, advocating for underlying interests rather than rigid positions, prioritizing effectiveness over the need to be right, and seeking behavior changes rather than personality transformations. Adopting these shifts can create a more constructive and productive environment for resolving conflicts and fostering better communication.

4 mental shifts
that make it easier to have a
Difficult Conversation

"Difficult person" ➡	"Difficult situation"
Advocating for your position ➡	Advocating for your interests
Be proven right ➡	Be effective
Change their personality/style ➡	Change their behavior

1. Shifting from focusing on a difficult person to understanding a complex situation allows you to detach personal feelings and biases, enabling a more objective assessment of the circumstances. Recognizing that both parties are reasonable individuals caught in challenging circumstances opens up possibilities for collaborative problem-solving rather than fixating on personal differences.

2. Moving from advocating for positions to advocating for underlying interests promotes a deeper understanding of the motivations and needs driving each party's stance. By identifying the core interests and goals behind differing positions, you can explore creative solutions that address those

interests while maintaining a sense of fairness and mutual benefit.

3. Shifting from a mindset of proving oneself right to being effective emphasizes the importance of achieving desired outcomes over winning arguments. Instead of focusing solely on asserting correctness, prioritize finding practical solutions that meet the needs of all parties involved. This shift enables greater flexibility, cooperation, and the potential for long-term relationship building.

4. Moving from desiring a change in personality to seeking a behavior change recognizes the limitations of altering someone's innate disposition. Instead, concentrate on influencing specific actions and behaviors that are causing difficulties. By framing the requested behavior change as advantageous to the individual, you also increase the chances of them being receptive to the proposed modifications while maintaining a sense of respect.

Common Challenges and Barriers to Effective Communication

Effective communication is the lifeblood of successful leadership. It forms the foundation for building strong relationships, resolving conflicts, and fostering collaboration within teams and organizations. However, when engaging in difficult conversations with challenging personalities, leaders often encounter a myriad of challenges and barriers that impede effective communication. In this section, we will examine some common obstacles encountered during difficult conversations, highlighting the factors that impede productive dialogue. By understanding these challenges, leaders can proactively address them, enhance their communication skills, and pave the way for more successful outcomes.

Emotional Intensity

One of the primary challenges in difficult conversations is the heightened emotional intensity they often carry. Emotions such as anger, frustration, fear, or defensiveness can cloud judgment, hinder effective listening, and escalate conflicts. When individuals feel threatened or personally attacked, they may become reactive and less receptive to different perspectives. Managing our own emotions and those of others is vital for maintaining a calm and constructive atmosphere. It requires leaders to cultivate emotional intelligence, self-awareness, and the ability to regulate their own emotions while empathizing with the emotions of others.

Lack of Trust

Trust forms the bedrock of effective communication, but can be eroded in difficult conversations. Previous negative experiences, conflicts, or strained relationships can create a lack of trust between individuals, leading to defensiveness, skepticism, and reluctance to engage openly. Establishing and rebuilding trust requires consistent authenticity, transparency, and demonstrating a genuine concern for the well-being and perspectives of others. Leaders must work diligently to foster an environment of psychological safety where individuals feel comfortable expressing their thoughts and concerns without fear of judgment or reprisal.

Misaligned Expectations and Assumptions

Misaligned expectations and assumptions are frequent barriers to effective communication. Individuals may enter a conversation with varying assumptions, perspectives, and preconceived notions, which can lead to misunderstandings and misinterpretations. These assumptions can stem from differences in communication styles, cultural backgrounds, or past experiences. Leaders must be mindful of these potential gaps and actively seek to clarify expectations, validate assumptions, and promote a shared understanding. This state can be achieved through active listening, asking open-ended questions, and engaging in reflective dialogue to uncover and address misalignments.

_____

_____

_____

_____

Defensive Behaviors

In difficult conversations, it is common for individuals to exhibit defensive behaviors as a protective mechanism. Defensiveness may manifest as denial, blame shifting, avoidance, or counteraccusations. These behaviors hinder progress and prevent meaningful communication from taking place. As leaders, it is essential to approach difficult conversations with empathy and non-judgment, creating a safe space where individuals feel heard and validated. By focusing on the underlying interests, needs, and motivations of all parties involved, leaders can help diffuse defensiveness and foster a collaborative approach to problem-solving.

_____

_____

_____

Power Imbalances

Power imbalances can pose significant barriers to effective communication, particularly in hierarchical organizations. When one party holds more authority or perceived power, it can hinder open dialogue, suppress the expression of differing opinions, and result in an unequal distribution of influence. Leaders must be aware of their positional power and strive to create a level playing field where everyone's voice is valued and heard. Actively soliciting input, encouraging diverse perspectives, and practicing inclusive decision-making processes can help mitigate the impact of power imbalances.

Navigating difficult conversations with challenging personalities requires an awareness of the common challenges and barriers that impede effective communication. Leaders can overcome these obstacles by understanding the emotional intensity, cultivating trust, addressing misaligned expectations, managing defensive behaviors, mitigating power imbalances, and creating an environment conducive to productive dialogue. Investing in the development of practical communication skills empowers leaders to build stronger relationships, foster collaboration, and drive positive change within their teams and organizations.

Exploring Impacts of Unresolved Issues

Unresolved issues stemming from difficult conversations with challenging personalities can have far-reaching effects on individuals and organizations. When conflicts, grievances, or sensitive topics are left unaddressed, they can fester, perpetuate negative dynamics, and hinder personal and professional growth. This section will delve into the personal and organizational impacts of unresolved issues, highlighting the importance of proactively addressing them. By understanding the consequences of leaving issues unresolved, leaders can recognize the urgency of engaging in difficult conversations and seek strategies for effective resolution.

_____

_____

_____

Personal Impacts

Unresolved issues can have profound personal impacts on individuals involved in difficult conversations. Firstly, these issues can increase stress and anxiety, affecting mental and emotional well-being. The constant tension and worry associated with unresolved conflicts can affect individuals' overall productivity, motivation, and job satisfaction.

_____

_____

_____

Additionally, unresolved issues can strain relationships and erode trust among team members. Unaddressed conflicts can escalate, leading to breakdowns in communication, collaboration, and teamwork. This situation affects the individuals directly involved and creates a toxic work environment that can permeate the entire organization.

_____

_____

_____

Unresolved issues can also hinder personal growth and development. When difficult conversations are avoided or handled ineffectively, opportunities for learning, self-reflection, and skill enhancement are missed. Individuals may struggle to identify areas for improvement or fail to gain insights into their blind spots and limitations. Consequently, personal and professional growth may be stunted, hindering career advancement and success.

Organizational Impacts

Unresolved issues can have a significant impact on individuals and have substantial consequences for the organization. Firstly, they can lead to a decline in productivity and efficiency. When conflicts or disagreements persist without resolution, the energy that could be channeled into productive work is diverted toward ongoing tension and disputes. This concept can result in a decrease in overall output, missed deadlines, and compromised work quality.

Moreover, unresolved issues can harm employee morale and engagement. A toxic work environment characterized by unresolved conflicts, strained relationships, and a lack of trust can lead to decreased job satisfaction and increased turnover. Disengaged employees may feel demotivated, disconnected, and undervalued, which can have a ripple effect on team dynamics and overall organizational culture.

Unresolved issues can also impede effective decision-making and problem-solving within the organization. When conflicts or differing viewpoints go unaddressed, they can lead to biases, information silos, and suboptimal outcomes. The lack of open and honest communication can hinder the sharing of diverse perspectives, creative problem-solving, and innovation.

Addressing Unresolved Issues

Recognizing the personal and organizational impacts of unresolved issues highlights the urgency of engaging in difficult conversations. Leaders must take on the responsibility of facilitating constructive dialogue, creating a safe space for open communication, and promoting the resolution of conflicts. By proactively addressing these issues, leaders can foster a healthier work environment, strengthen relationships, and enhance organizational performance.

Leaders must develop the necessary skills to navigate difficult conversations effectively, such as active listening, empathy, and conflict resolution. They must foster a culture of open communication, where individuals feel empowered to express concerns, provide feedback, and collaborate on finding solutions. Implementing formal channels for conflict resolution, such as mediation or facilitated discussions, can also contribute to a more proactive approach to addressing unresolved issues.

Unresolved issues stemming from difficult conversations with challenging personalities can have a profound impact on individuals and organizations. The personal implications range from increased stress and strained relationships to hindered personal growth and development. At the organizational level, unresolved issues can lead to decreased productivity, low morale, and compromised decision-making. By recognizing the consequences of leaving issues unresolved, leaders can proactively engage in difficult conversations, seek resolution, and create a positive and productive work environment. Taking the initiative to address these issues promotes personal well-being, strengthens relationships, and drives organizational success.

Preparing for Difficult Conversations

Preparing for difficult conversations is a vital step in ensuring a productive outcome. It requires a thoughtful and strategic approach that encompasses self-awareness and careful planning. In this section, we will examine the factors that contribute to assessing the need for a difficult conversation, including the importance of addressing the issue and the potential consequences of avoidance. Additionally, we will explore the importance of recognizing our personal triggers and developing emotional intelligence to navigate challenging situations with composure and clarity. By setting clear goals and planning for success, we can enter difficult conversations equipped with the tools to navigate them effectively.

Assessing the Need for a Conversation

Engaging in difficult conversations with challenging personalities requires careful consideration and assessment of the need for such conversations. While difficult conversations can be challenging, they are often essential for resolving conflicts, addressing concerns, and fostering growth. This section will explore the importance of assessing the need for a conversation before initiating it. By understanding the significance of this assessment, leaders can make informed decisions about when and how to engage in difficult conversations, ensuring the best possible outcomes.

Understanding the Importance of Assessment

Before embarking on a difficult conversation, it is essential to assess whether it is necessary or beneficial to have the conversation at all. Assessing the need for a conversation helps leaders evaluate the potential impact, weigh the risks and benefits, and determine the most effective approach to addressing the issue. Without a thoughtful assessment, leaders may engage in unnecessary or unproductive conversations, wasting valuable time and energy.

Factors to Consider in the Assessment

Relevance and Significance of the Issue: Leaders should evaluate the relevance and significance of the issue they plan to address. Is it a pressing concern that directly impacts individuals or the organization? Does it align with the organization's values, goals, or priorities? Assessing the issue's importance helps determine whether a conversation is warranted and whether it merits immediate attention.

Potential Impact on Individuals and the Organization: Consider the potential impact of the unresolved issue on the individuals involved and the overall organizational dynamics. Will the issue continue to escalate if left unaddressed? Are there potential consequences for productivity, morale, or teamwork? Assessing the potential impact helps gauge the urgency and necessity of initiating a difficult conversation.

Availability of Alternative Solutions: Leaders should consider whether there are alternative approaches or solutions to the issue that do not require a difficult conversation. Are there mediation or conflict resolution techniques that can be employed? Can the issue be addressed indirectly through policy changes or team-building activities? Evaluating the availability of alternative solutions helps determine whether a conversation is the most appropriate and effective course of action.

Willingness and Readiness of the Parties Involved: Assessing the willingness and readiness of all parties involved in the conversation is crucial. Are they open to engaging in a dialogue? Do they demonstrate a genuine interest in resolving the issue? Willing and receptive participants are more likely to contribute constructively to the conversation, leading to more positive outcomes. If parties are unwilling or unready, it may be necessary to postpone or approach the conversation in a different manner.

The balance between Immediate Need and Emotional Readiness: Timing plays a significant role in the success of a difficult conversation. Leaders must assess whether there is an immediate need for the conversation or if it can be postponed, allowing for emotional readiness and preparation. Sometimes, emotions may be too high, or individuals may not be in the right mindset to engage effectively. Assessing the balance between immediate need and emotional readiness helps determine the optimal timing for the conversation.

Assessing the need for a difficult conversation is crucial in effective leadership. By evaluating the relevance and significance of the issue, the potential impact on individuals and the organization, the availability of alternative solutions, the willingness and readiness of the parties involved, and the balance between immediate need and emotional readiness, leaders can make informed decisions about whether to proceed with a conversation. This assessment ensures that leaders invest their time, energy, and resources in necessary conversations in a timely manner and have the potential to yield positive outcomes. By approaching difficult conversations with intention and thoughtful assessment, leaders can navigate them more effectively and promote growth, understanding, and resolution within their teams and organizations.

_____

_____

_____

_____

Identifying Personal Triggers and Emotional Intelligence

Difficult conversations with challenging personalities can evoke strong emotions and test our ability to communicate effectively. Leaders must identify their triggers and develop emotional intelligence to navigate these challenging interactions with composure, empathy, and a constructive mindset. In this section, we will examine the importance of recognizing personal triggers and developing emotional intelligence in challenging conversations. By gaining insights into our emotional responses and enhancing our emotional intelligence, leaders can approach difficult conversations with greater self-awareness, empathy, and effectiveness.

Identifying Personal Triggers

Personal triggers are specific stimuli or situations that evoke strong emotional responses within individuals. They vary widely and are often rooted in past experiences, insecurities, or deeply held beliefs. When engaged in complex conversations, these triggers can lead to emotional reactivity, defensiveness, or a loss of clarity of thought. Therefore, identifying personal triggers is crucial for self-awareness and emotional regulation.

One way to identify personal triggers is through self-reflection and introspection. By examining our emotional responses in different situations, we can gain insights into the underlying triggers that evoke those reactions. Pay attention to patterns, recurring emotions, and physical sensations during difficult conversations.

Identifying personal triggers empowers leaders to recognize when they are being activated, enabling them to respond more consciously and thoughtfully.

Cultivating Emotional Intelligence

Emotional intelligence, often referred to as EQ, is the ability to recognize, understand, and manage our own emotions and the emotions of others. In the context of difficult conversations, emotional intelligence plays a vital role in fostering effective communication, empathy, and conflict resolution.

Self-Awareness

Self-awareness is the foundation of emotional intelligence. It involves recognizing our own emotions, strengths, weaknesses, and triggers. By developing self-awareness, leaders can recognize how their emotions impact their thoughts, behaviors, and communication styles during challenging conversations. This awareness enables a more intentional and controlled response, rather than reacting impulsively to emotional triggers.

Empathy

Empathy is the ability to understand and share the feelings of others. It is a key component of emotional intelligence when engaging with challenging personalities. By practicing empathy, leaders can put themselves in others' shoes, recognizing their perspectives, concerns, and emotions. This understanding helps create a more collaborative and respectful environment for dialogue, fostering a sense of trust and openness.

Emotional Regulation

Emotional regulation involves managing and controlling one's own emotions in various situations. During difficult conversations, emotions can run high, making it essential for leaders to regulate their emotional responses. This regulation enables leaders to maintain their composure, think clearly, and respond in a manner that is constructive and conducive to productive dialogue. Techniques such as deep breathing, mindfulness, and self-reflection can aid in emotional regulation.

Active Listening

Active listening is a fundamental aspect of emotional intelligence. It involves fully engaging in the conversation, attentively listening to others, and validating their experiences and perspectives. By practicing active listening, leaders can demonstrate empathy, gain a deeper understanding of the other person's perspective, and foster trust and respect.

Identifying personal triggers and developing emotional intelligence are essential skills for leaders engaging in difficult conversations with challenging personalities. Leaders can navigate these conversations with greater self-awareness, empathy, and control by understanding their emotional responses and cultivating emotional intelligence. Recognizing personal triggers allows leaders to respond more thoughtfully and effectively. At the same time, emotional intelligence promotes effective communication, empathy, and conflict resolution. These skills enable leaders to cultivate healthier relationships, navigate conflicts effectively, and foster a positive and productive work environment.

Goal Setting and Planning for Successful Outcomes

Engaging in difficult conversations with challenging personalities can be challenging and unpredictable. Leaders must set clear goals and engage in thoughtful planning to navigate these conversations effectively. Goal setting provides direction and purpose, while planning enables leaders to anticipate potential challenges and strategize for successful outcomes. In this section, we will examine the significance of goal setting and planning in the context of challenging conversations. By establishing clear objectives and formulating a comprehensive plan, leaders can approach these conversations with confidence, focus, and a higher likelihood of achieving positive results.

Setting Clear Goals

Setting clear goals is a fundamental step in preparing for difficult conversations. Clear goals provide a sense of direction and purpose, helping leaders stay focused and on track during the conversation. When establishing goals, it is crucial to consider the desired outcomes and the specific issues that need to be addressed. Clear goals help guide the conversation, create alignment among participants, and provide a framework for evaluating success.

Some key considerations when setting goals for difficult conversations include:

1. **Clarity:** Goals should be clear and specific, leaving no room for ambiguity. Clearly articulate the issues to be addressed, the outcomes desired, and any specific actions or resolutions that need to be achieved.

   _____

   _____

2. **Realistic Expectations:** Set realistic expectations for the conversation. Recognize that difficult conversations may not always lead to a complete resolution or immediate change. Goals should be achievable within the context of the conversation and the relationship dynamics involved.

   _____

   _____

3. **Focus on Collaboration and Understanding: Shift** the focus of the goals from winning or proving a point to collaboration, understanding, and finding common ground. Emphasize creating a safe space for open dialogue and fostering mutual understanding.

   _____

   _____

4. **Long-Term Relationship Building:** Consider the long-term implications of the conversation on the relationship. Goals should aim to maintain or improve the relationship, even if the complete resolution of the issue is impossible. Strive for mutual respect, trust, and ongoing dialogue.

   _____

   _____

Planning for Successful Outcomes

Effective planning is crucial for achieving successful outcomes in challenging conversations. It involves anticipating potential challenges, considering different perspectives, and strategizing for constructive dialogue. A well-thought-out plan enables leaders to navigate complex dynamics and maintain control over the conversation, while fostering an environment conducive to open communication.

Key elements of planning for successful outcomes include:

1. **Preparation**: Thoroughly prepare for the conversation by gathering relevant information, understanding the different viewpoints, and considering potential objections or pushbacks. Anticipate potential emotional triggers and plan strategies to remain composed and focused.

2. **Structuring the Conversation:** Develop a clear structure for the conversation to ensure it flows smoothly. Outline the topics to discuss, identify key points, and plan for appropriate timing. A structured conversation helps maintain focus, prevents tangents, and addresses relevant aspects.

3. **Active Listening and Empathy:** Plan to actively listen to the other person's perspective and demonstrate empathy. Consider potential questions or prompts that can encourage others to share their thoughts and feelings openly. Actively listening and empathizing help foster respectful and constructive dialogue.

4. **Conflict Resolution Strategies:** Plan for potential conflicts or disagreements that may arise during the conversation. Consider conflict resolution strategies such as reframing, finding common ground, or seeking compromise. Prepare

responses to challenging or defensive behaviors, ensuring the conversation stays on track and progresses toward resolution.

5. **Post-Conversation Follow-up: Plan** for post-conversation follow-up to ensure that progress continues beyond the initial conversation. Determine appropriate next steps, whether it involves further discussion, implementation of agreed-upon actions, or ongoing support. Follow-up reinforces the commitment to resolution and maintains accountability.

Setting clear goals and engaging in thoughtful planning are crucial steps in preparing for difficult conversations with challenging personalities. Clear goals provide direction and purpose, while planning helps anticipate challenges and strategize for successful outcomes.

By establishing clear objectives, focusing on collaboration and understanding, and planning for effective communication and conflict resolution, leaders can approach difficult conversations with confidence and increase the likelihood of achieving positive results. Through goal setting and planning, leaders can navigate these conversations with purpose, resilience, and a commitment to fostering healthier relationships and organizational growth.

Strategies for Engaging Challenging Personalities

Engaging with challenging personalities can be a formidable challenge for leaders. However, with the right strategies and techniques, it is possible to establish constructive dialogue and foster understanding. This section will focus on active listening and empathy as foundational skills for engaging difficult individuals. By honing these skills, leaders can create an environment that encourages open communication and mutual respect. We will also explore techniques for recognizing and managing defensive behaviors, allowing for a more productive exchange of ideas and perspectives.

Ultimately, leaders can navigate challenging interactions with challenging personalities by building rapport and finding common ground more effectively.

Active Listening and Empathy

Engaging in difficult conversations with challenging personalities requires leaders to hone their active listening skills and cultivate empathy. Active listening and empathy are powerful tools that foster understanding, defuse tensions, and create an environment conducive to open and constructive dialogue. This section will examine the significance of active listening and empathy in challenging conversations. By developing these skills, leaders can establish rapport, build trust, and navigate challenging interactions with empathy, respect, and effectiveness.

The Power of Active Listening

Active listening is a foundational skill for effective communication, particularly in difficult conversations. It involves entirely focusing on and understanding the speaker's message, both verbal and non-verbal, without interrupting or imposing judgment. Active listening creates a safe space for individuals to express themselves, encourages trust, and promotes mutual respect. By actively listening, leaders can demonstrate their genuine interest in understanding the other person's perspective, fostering a more meaningful and productive exchange.

_____

_____

Key Elements of Active Listening

Full Attention: Give the speaker your undivided attention verbally and non-verbally. Maintain eye contact, avoid distractions, and refrain from interrupting or formulating responses in your mind while the other person is speaking. Demonstrate your full presence and engagement through your body language and demeanor.

_____

_____

Non-Verbal Cues: Pay attention to the speaker's non-verbal cues, such as facial expressions, tone of voice, and body language. These cues can provide valuable insights into the emotions and underlying messages being conveyed. Acknowledge and respond to these cues to demonstrate empathy and understanding.

_____

_____

Clarification and Reflection: Seek clarification and paraphrase the speaker's message to ensure a clear and accurate understanding. Reflecting on what you have heard confirms and validates the speaker's thoughts and feelings. This practice also helps to clarify any misinterpretations or misunderstandings that may arise during the conversation.

_____

_____

_____

Cultivating Empathy

Empathy is the ability to understand and share another person's feelings, thoughts, and experiences. It is a powerful tool that helps bridge the gap between individuals and fosters an environment of trust and connection. Cultivating empathy enables leaders to see beyond their own perspectives and genuinely appreciate the emotions and concerns of others, even in challenging conversations.

Key Elements of Cultivating Empathy

1. **Perspective-taking: Put yourself in the other person's shoes and strive to understand their perspective.** Recognize that everyone brings unique experiences, values, and beliefs to the conversation. By actively considering their perspective, you can cultivate empathy and foster a deeper understanding of their emotions and motivations.

2. **Non-Judgmental Attitude:** Approach the conversation with a non-judgmental attitude, suspending assumptions and biases. Avoid labeling or categorizing others based on their behavior or opinions. Embrace an open mindset that allows for genuine curiosity and a willingness to learn from their perspective.

3. **Validation and Recognition:** Validate the other person's emotions and experiences by acknowledging and recognizing their feelings. Show empathy through verbal and non-verbal cues, such as nodding, maintaining eye contact, or offering

understanding words. Validating emotions creates an atmosphere of acceptance and trust.

_____

_____

_____

4. **Emotional Regulation:** Maintain emotional regulation during difficult conversations by managing your own emotions and responding with composure and restraint. Staying calm and composed creates a safe space for others to express themselves openly without fear of judgment or retaliation. Emotional regulation also allows for clearer thinking and more effective communication.

_____

_____

_____

Active listening and empathy are essential skills for leaders engaging in difficult conversations with individuals who have challenging personalities. By actively listening, leaders demonstrate their commitment to understanding and validating the other person's perspective, fostering trust and rapport.

Cultivating empathy enables leaders to connect on a deeper level, appreciate the emotions and experiences of others, and create an environment of respect and understanding. By integrating active listening and empathy into their communication toolkit, leaders can navigate difficult conversations with greater ease, empathy, and effectiveness, thereby improving relationships, collaboration, and overall organizational success.

Recognizing and Managing Defensive Behaviors

When engaging in difficult conversations with challenging personalities, it is common for defensive behaviors to arise. Defensiveness can hinder effective communication, escalate conflicts, and impede resolution. As leaders, it is crucial to recognize and manage defensive behaviors in ourselves and others, creating an environment conducive to open dialogue and productive outcomes. This section will examine the significance of acknowledging and addressing defensive behaviors during challenging conversations. Leaders can foster a more collaborative and constructive approach to resolving conflicts by developing strategies to address defensiveness and promote open communication.

Recognizing Defensive Behaviors

Recognizing defensive behaviors is a critical first step in managing them effectively. Defensive behaviors manifest in various ways, often as a protective response to perceived threats or criticism. Some common defensive behaviors include:

1. **Denial:** Individuals may deny or dismiss any responsibility or involvement in the issue. They may refuse to acknowledge their role or the impact of their actions, deflecting blame onto others or external factors.

2. **Counter-Attacking:** When individuals feel threatened, they may respond by launching personal attacks or criticisms against others involved in the conversation. They may attempt to divert

attention from the issue by shifting blame or focusing on unrelated matters.

3. **Avoidance:** Individuals may try to evade or avoid the conversation altogether. They may change the subject, make excuses, or withdraw from the interaction to protect themselves from uncomfortable emotions or confrontations.

4. **Justifying or Rationalizing:** Individuals may employ extensive explanations, justifications, or rationalizations to justify their actions or positions. They may use logical reasoning or provide excuses to defend their behaviors, seeking to protect their self-image or maintain their perceived correctness.

Managing Defensive Behaviors

Effectively managing defensive behaviors requires a mindful and empathetic approach. By employing effective strategies, leaders can foster a safe and supportive environment that promotes open dialogue and constructive problem-solving. Here are some strategies to consider:

1. **Foster Psychological Safety:** Establish an atmosphere of psychological safety where individuals feel comfortable expressing their thoughts and concerns without fear of judgment or retribution. Establish clear ground rules that foster respect, active listening, and open-mindedness.

2. **Active Listening and Validation:** Practice active listening and validate the feelings and perspectives of others. Demonstrate empathy by acknowledging their emotions and making them feel heard and understood. This action can help reduce defensiveness and create a more receptive environment for collaboration.

_____

_____

3. **Seek Understanding:** Instead of focusing on blame or fault, aim to understand the underlying motivations and concerns of the person displaying defensive behaviors. Ask open-ended questions and encourage them to share their thoughts and feelings without interruption. This approach can help uncover root causes and promote empathy and understanding.

_____

_____

4. **Reframe and Redirect:** When faced with defensive behaviors, reframe the conversation by highlighting common goals, shared interests, or areas of agreement. Redirect the focus towards finding mutually beneficial solutions and fostering collaboration rather than dwelling on individual positions.

_____

_____

5. Role Model Non-Defensive Behavior: As a leader, model non-defensive behavior in your actions and responses. Stay calm, composed, and open-minded, even in the face of defensiveness. By setting an example of constructive dialogue and vulnerability, you encourage others to do the same.

_____

_____

_____

6. Provide Constructive Feedback: When necessary, provide feedback on the defensive behaviors exhibited by others. Be specific, non-judgmental, and focus on the impact of the behavior rather than attacking the individual. Suggest alternative approaches to promote more effective communication and conflict resolution.

_____

_____

_____

Recognizing and managing defensive behaviors is crucial for effective leadership during difficult conversations with challenging personalities. By being attentive to defensive behaviors, leaders can respond with empathy, create a psychologically safe environment, and foster an atmosphere conducive to open dialogue and collaboration. Through active listening, validation, seeking understanding, reframing, role modeling, and providing constructive feedback, leaders can help mitigate defensiveness and promote more productive and constructive interactions. By addressing defensiveness, leaders can pave the way for meaningful resolution, stronger relationships, and a healthier organizational culture.

_____

_____

_____

Building Rapport and Establishing Common Ground

Building rapport and establishing common ground are essential components of having successful, yet tricky, conversations with challenging personalities. When faced with challenging interactions, leaders must prioritize relationship-building and finding areas of agreement to create a foundation for productive dialogue. This section will examine the significance of building rapport and establishing common ground in challenging conversations. By fostering a sense of connection and shared understanding, leaders can navigate these conversations with empathy, respect, and a higher likelihood of achieving mutually beneficial outcomes.

The Power of Rapport

Rapport refers to a harmonious relationship or connection between individuals. Building rapport during challenging conversations is crucial for establishing trust, openness, and a sense of mutual respect. Individuals who feel a genuine connection are more likely to engage in meaningful dialogue, share perspectives, and work towards finding common ground. Rapport-building sets the stage for collaborative problem-solving and positive outcomes.

Strategies for Building Rapport:

1. **Active Listening:** Demonstrate active listening by giving your full attention to the other person. Listen without interrupting, show genuine interest, and respond with empathy and understanding. You create a sense of rapport and validation by actively engaging in the conversation and valuing the other person's input.

   _____

   _____

2. **Find Common Interests or Experiences:** Look for common interests, experiences, or values that can serve as a foundation for building rapport. These shared aspects create a sense of connection, enabling individuals to relate to one another on a deeper level. Establishing common ground helps to bridge potential gaps and facilitates a more productive dialogue.

   _____

   _____

Empathy and Understanding: Cultivate empathy by putting yourself in the other person's shoes and seeking to understand their perspective. Validate their emotions and experiences, even if you may disagree with their position. Demonstrating empathy fosters rapport by showing that you genuinely care about their feelings and concerns.

Respectful Communication: Maintain a respectful and positive tone throughout the conversation. Use inclusive language, avoid personal attacks, and focus on the issue at hand rather than attacking the person. You foster a respectful communication style by creating an environment that encourages openness, trust, and a sense of rapport.

_____

_____

_____

Establishing Common Ground

Establishing common ground is crucial for finding areas of agreement and shared objectives in difficult conversations. It helps to create a foundation for collaboration, build trust, and work toward a mutually beneficial resolution. By identifying shared interests or goals, leaders can navigate differences more effectively and foster a sense of teamwork.

Strategies for Establishing Common Ground:

1. **Identify Shared Objectives:** Identify shared objectives or goals that both parties can work towards. Emphasize the mutual benefits and positive outcomes that can be achieved by finding common ground. Individuals can align their efforts and collaborate more effectively by focusing on shared objectives.

   _____

   _____

2. **Highlight Overlapping Interests:** Explore areas of overlapping interests or concerns. Find common values or priorities that both parties can agree upon. You can shift the conversation towards finding solutions that address the shared concerns by highlighting these commonalities.

3. **Seek Win-Win Solutions:** Encourage a collaborative mindset by seeking win-win solutions. Emphasize that the goal is not to "win" the conversation or overpower the other person but to find a resolution that meets the needs and interests of both parties. Common ground can be established more effectively by fostering a sense of cooperation and shared success.

4. **Emphasize Open Dialogue:** Promote open dialogue and invite diverse perspectives. Encourage all parties to share their thoughts, concerns, and ideas without fear of judgment or criticism. By fostering a safe space for open dialogue, you create an environment that values different viewpoints and promotes the exploration of common ground.

Building rapport and establishing common ground are vital to engaging in difficult conversations with challenging personalities. Leaders can foster a sense of connection and trust by prioritizing relationship-building, active listening, empathy, and respectful communication. By identifying shared objectives, highlighting overlapping interests, and seeking mutually beneficial solutions, leaders can establish common ground and lay the groundwork for collaborative problem-solving. Through these strategies, leaders can navigate difficult conversations with empathy, respect, and a focus on finding mutually beneficial outcomes, ultimately fostering stronger relationships, increased understanding, and positive organizational growth.

Effective Communication Techniques

Effective communication is at the core of successful leadership, particularly when it comes to difficult conversations. This section will explore communication techniques to help leaders convey their message clearly, assertively, and empathetically. We will examine the importance of maintaining a balance between being direct and respectful, as well as managing non-verbal cues and body language, to enhance communication effectiveness. Furthermore, we will explore the intricacies of handling conflict and negotiating win-win solutions, thereby fostering an environment that encourages collaboration and resolution.

Straightforward and assertive communication is vital when engaging in difficult conversations with challenging personalities. It enables leaders to articulate their thoughts, concerns, and boundaries effectively, fostering understanding and promoting constructive dialogue. This section will examine the significance of clear and assertive communication in challenging conversations. By mastering this skill, leaders can navigate challenging interactions with confidence, respect, and a higher likelihood of achieving positive outcomes.

The Power of Clear Communication

Clear communication is the cornerstone of effective leadership and successful difficult conversations. It involves expressing ideas, expectations, and concerns concisely, directly, and unambiguously. Clear communication ensures that messages are understood and minimizes misunderstandings, confusion, or misinterpretations. When leaders communicate clearly, they provide a solid foundation for productive dialogue and problem-solving.

Strategies for Clear Communication:

5. **Use Concise and Specific Language:** Choose words and phrases that are clear, concise, and specific. Avoid using ambiguous or vague language that can lead to misinterpretations. Be mindful of your tone and ensure your message aligns with your intended meaning.

    _____

    _____

6. **Focus on the Issue, Not the Person:** Direct your communication towards the specific issue at hand rather than attacking or criticizing the person. Frame your thoughts and concerns in a way that separates the behavior or situation from the individual, fostering a more productive and respectful conversation.

    _____

    _____

7. **Use Active Listening and Confirmation:** Engage in active listening by attentively and actively processing the information the other person shares. Confirm your understanding by paraphrasing or summarizing their message to ensure accuracy. This idea demonstrates your commitment to clear and accurate communication.

    _____

    _____

8. **Seek Clarification:** Do not hesitate to ask questions if you are unsure about something or need further clarification. Seeking

clarification helps prevent assumptions and misunderstandings, ensuring that everyone is on the same page. Encourage the other person to provide clarification as well to promote mutual understanding.

_____

_____

_____

The Importance of Assertive Communication

Assertive communication is crucial when engaging in difficult conversations. It allows leaders to express their thoughts, needs, and boundaries directly and respectfully while actively listening to others. Assertive communication helps set clear expectations, establish boundaries, and foster open and honest dialogue.

_____

_____

_____

Strategies for Assertive Communication

1. Use "I" Statements: When expressing your thoughts or concerns, use "I" statements to take ownership of your feelings and opinions. This approach helps to avoid sounding accusatory or confrontational. For example, say, "I feel..." or "I believe..." instead of using "you" statements that can come across as blaming.

_____

_____

2. **Express Boundaries and Expectations:** Clearly communicate your boundaries and expectations regarding behavior, actions, or outcomes. Be assertive in expressing what you are willing to accept or not. This communication style helps establish mutual

respect and allows for a common understanding of each person's limits.

_____

_____

3. **Maintain Calm and Composure:** Stay calm and composed during the conversation, even if the other person becomes defensive or confrontational. Maintain a confident and respectful tone, and avoid becoming reactive or aggressive. Calmness can help de-escalate tense situations and promote a more productive exchange.

_____

_____

4. **Practice Active Listening and Empathy:** While assertively expressing your thoughts and concerns, also practice active listening and empathy. Give the other person the opportunity to share their perspective and genuinely try to understand their point of view. Demonstrating empathy creates a more conducive environment for open dialogue and problem-solving.

_____

_____

Straightforward and assertive communication is fundamental when engaging in difficult conversations with challenging personalities. By mastering this skill, leaders can effectively convey their thoughts, concerns, and boundaries, thereby fostering understanding and respect. Through clear communication, leaders establish a foundation for productive dialogue and minimize misunderstandings.

_____

_____

_____

Leaders can express themselves confidently, set boundaries, and maintain respectful interactions through assertive communication. By integrating clear and assertive communication strategies, leaders can confidently navigate difficult conversations, promote understanding, and work towards positive outcomes, ultimately fostering stronger relationships, collaboration, and organizational growth.

Managing Non-Verbal Cues and Body Language

Nonverbal cues and body language are crucial in communication, particularly during difficult conversations with challenging personalities. Leaders must be aware of and manage their own non-verbal cues while also interpreting and responding to the non-verbal cues of others. This section will examine the significance of managing nonverbal cues and body language in challenging conversations. By effectively understanding and utilizing these cues, leaders can enhance communication, build rapport, and navigate challenging interactions with greater success.

The Impact of Non-Verbal Cues and Body Language

Non-verbal cues and body language convey powerful messages that can complement, contradict, or reinforce spoken words. They often reveal underlying emotions, attitudes, and intentions that may not be explicitly expressed. In difficult conversations, being attuned to non-verbal cues is essential for understanding the true meaning behind the words and fostering a more comprehensive and empathetic exchange.

Managing Non-Verbal Cues

1. **Facial Expressions:** Pay attention to your facial expressions, as they can convey a range of emotions. Practice maintaining a neutral or calm expression, even if the conversation becomes challenging. This concept can help create an atmosphere of open dialogue and prevent potential escalation of conflicts.

2. **Eye Contact:** Maintain appropriate eye contact with the other person. Avoid staring or looking away excessively, as this may be perceived as confrontational or disinterested. Sustaining eye contact demonstrates attentiveness and respect.

3. **Posture and Gestures:** Be mindful of your posture and body language, including your gestures. Adopt an open and relaxed posture, avoiding crossed arms or defensive postures. Use appropriate gestures that enhance your message and show engagement, but be mindful of excessive or distracting movements.

4. **Voice Tone and Volume:** Pay attention to your tone and volume of voice. Speak clearly and project your voice effectively, ensuring your message is both audible and easily understood. Use a tone that conveys respect and avoids coming across as aggressive or dismissive.

_____

_____

_____

Interpreting and Responding to Non-Verbal Cues

1. **Active Observation:** Observe the nonverbal cues of the other person actively. Please pay attention to their facial expressions, body language, and tone of voice. These cues can provide valuable insights into their emotional state and help you adjust your approach accordingly.

_____

_____

2. **Seek Clarification:** If you notice conflicting verbal and non-verbal cues, seek clarification better to understand the other person's intentions or emotions. Ask open-ended questions or paraphrase their message to confirm your understanding of it. This process demonstrates your attentiveness and willingness to engage in a genuine conversation.

_____

_____

3. **Adjust Your Approach:** Use the nonverbal cues of the other person to guide your responses and adjust your approach accordingly. Consider adopting a more empathetic and supportive stance if they appear defensive or guarded. If they seem receptive, maintain a respectful and assertive tone in your communication style.

_____

_____

4. **Empathy and Validation:** Demonstrate empathy and validation through your non-verbal cues. Use appropriate facial

expressions, nodding, and other gestures to show understanding and support. This clarification can help create a safe space for others to express themselves openly.

_____

_____

_____

Managing non-verbal cues and body language is crucial for effective communication in difficult conversations. By being mindful of non-verbal cues and responding sensitively to the cues of others, leaders can enhance their understanding, build rapport, and navigate challenging interactions more successfully. Non-verbal cues offer valuable insights into emotions, intentions, and underlying messages that may not be explicitly expressed. Leaders can foster a more comprehensive and empathetic exchange by leveraging these cues, leading to increased understanding, collaboration, and positive outcomes in difficult conversations.

_____

_____

_____

_____

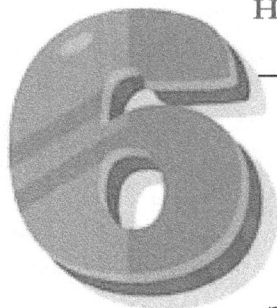

Handling Conflict and Negotiating Win-Win Solutions

Difficult conversations with challenging personalities often involve conflict and differing viewpoints. Leaders must develop skills in handling conflict effectively and finding win-win solutions that address the needs and interests of all parties involved. By approaching conflicts with a constructive mindset and employing negotiation techniques, leaders can navigate these challenging situations, promote understanding, and achieve resolutions that benefit everyone. This section will explore strategies for handling conflict and negotiating win-win solutions under challenging conversations.

Understanding Conflict

Conflict arises when there are differences in opinions, goals, or interests. In difficult conversations, conflicts can escalate if not managed properly. It is essential to recognize that conflict is a natural and inevitable aspect of human interactions. By viewing conflict as an opportunity for growth and positive change, leaders can approach it with a proactive and solution-oriented mindset.

Handling Conflict Effectively

1. **Foster Open Communication:** Create an environment that encourages open communication, where all parties feel safe expressing their concerns and opinions. Encourage active listening, empathetic understanding, and mutual respect. By fostering open communication, you lay the foundation for productive conflict resolution.

2. **Identify Underlying Interests:** Look beyond the surface-level positions and identify the underlying interests of each party involved. Understanding all parties' motivations, needs, and concerns can help find common ground and generate creative solutions that address those underlying interests.

   _____

   _____

   _____

3. **Seek Collaborative Solutions: Shift** the focus from a win-lose mindset to a collaborative approach. Aim to find solutions that satisfy the interests of all parties involved—collaborative solutions foster cooperation and mutual benefit, resulting in longer-lasting and more sustainable resolutions.

   _____

   _____

   _____

4. **Practice Effective Problem-Solving:** Utilize effective problem-solving techniques, such as brainstorming or evaluating alternative solutions. Encourage the generation of multiple ideas and perspectives. Facilitate a collaborative discussion where all parties can contribute their insights and potential solutions.

   _____

   _____

   _____

Negotiating Win-Win Solutions

1. **Establish Common Goals:** Identify common goals or objectives that all parties can agree upon. Emphasize shared

interests and areas of agreement. Establishing common ground creates a foundation for a collaborative negotiation process.

2. **Separate People from the Problem:** Focus on the problem rather than attacking or blaming individuals. Separate personal emotions from the conflict and address the underlying issues objectively. This approach allows for more productive and respectful discussions.

3. **Practice Active Listening and Empathy:** Listen actively and empathetically to the concerns and perspectives of all parties involved. Please demonstrate that you understand their viewpoints and validate their feelings. Active listening and empathy foster a sense of mutual understanding, facilitating effective negotiation.

4. **Explore Trade-offs and Compromises: Identify areas where trade-offs or compromises can be made to achieve a mutually beneficial** solution. Look for creative solutions that address the key interests of each party. Encourage flexibility and a willingness to find the middle ground.

5. **Use Objective Criteria:** Refer to objective criteria or standards to support your proposals and evaluate potential solutions. Objective criteria provide a basis for fairness and help

depersonalize the negotiation process. This approach increases the likelihood of finding mutually acceptable outcomes.

6. **Maintain Respectful Communication:** Ensure that communication remains respectful and constructive throughout the negotiation process. Use "I" statements, focus on the issues, and avoid personal attacks or confrontational language. Respectful communication fosters a positive atmosphere for negotiation.

Handling conflict and negotiating win-win solutions are essential skills for leaders engaging in difficult conversations with challenging personalities. Leaders can navigate conflicts effectively by fostering open communication, identifying underlying interests, and seeking collaborative solutions that benefit all parties. Through active listening, empathy, and a focus on shared goals, leaders can negotiate win-win solutions that address the needs and interests of all parties involved. By adopting these strategies, leaders can transform conflict into an opportunity for growth, promote understanding, and cultivate a positive and productive work environment.

Overcoming Resistance and Dealing with Difficult Personalities

In the realm of difficult conversations, resistance and difficult personalities can present significant challenges. This section will focus on strategies for overcoming resistance and navigating interactions with individuals who exhibit challenging behaviors. We will explore techniques for managing aggression and hostility, maintaining composure, and de-escalating tense situations. Additionally, we will address the complexities of managing passive-aggressive behaviors and offer strategies for addressing manipulation and power plays. By understanding and adapting to different personality types, leaders can approach challenging conversations with greater confidence and effectiveness.

Dealing with Aggression and Hostility

Engaging in difficult conversations with challenging personalities can sometimes escalate to aggression and hostility. As leaders, it is crucial to have strategies in place to manage and de-escalate these challenging situations effectively. By understanding the underlying causes of aggression and hostility and employing appropriate techniques, leaders can navigate these encounters with composure, assertiveness, and a focus on resolution. This section will explore strategies for managing aggression and hostility in challenging conversations, fostering a more productive and respectful exchange.

Understanding Aggression and Hostility

Aggression and hostility often stem from deep-seated emotions such as anger, frustration, or fear. In difficult conversations, individuals may resort to aggressive or hostile behavior as a defense mechanism, feeling threatened or challenged. It is essential to acknowledge that such behavior is typically a response to the situation, rather than a reflection of the leader's competence or character.

Dealing with Aggression and Hostility

1. **Stay Calm and Composed:** When faced with aggression or hostility, leaders must remain composed. Stay calm and composed, regulating your own emotions. Taking deep

breaths, practicing mindfulness, and using self-soothing techniques can help you remain centered and focused.

_____

_____

2. **Active Listening and Empathy:** Despite the hostile behavior, practice active listening and demonstrate empathy towards the other person. Allow them to express their concerns and frustrations without interruption. By actively listening and showing empathy, you can create an environment that encourages the person to feel heard and understood, potentially diffusing their aggression.

_____

_____

3. **Set Clear Boundaries:** Establish and clearly communicate acceptable behavior boundaries. Assertively and respectfully state that aggression and hostility will not be tolerated. Reinforce the expectation of respectful communication and assert your right to be treated respectfully.

_____

_____

4. **Use Assertive Communication:** Respond to aggression and hostility with assertive, yet respectful, communication. Clearly express your own thoughts, concerns, and boundaries in a calm and confident manner. Use "I" statements to convey your perspective without attacking or blaming the other person.

_____

_____

_____

5. **Reframe and Redirect:** Attempt to reframe the conversation by shifting the focus from personal attacks to the issue at hand. Redirect the conversation towards finding a solution or identifying common ground. Reframing and redirecting can steer the conversation to a more productive and respectful exchange.

_____

_____

6. **Take a Time-Out if Necessary:** Consider taking a time-out if the situation becomes overwhelming or unproductive. Politely suggest a break to allow both parties to cool down and regroup. This suggestion can help prevent the escalation of aggression and provide an opportunity to resume the conversation with a clearer mindset.

_____

_____

7. **Involve a Mediator or Neutral Third Party:** If the aggression and hostility persist, consider involving a mediator or neutral third party to facilitate the conversation. A mediator can help maintain a neutral and objective perspective, guiding the discussion toward a resolution while ensuring a safe and respectful environment.

_____

_____

8. **Prioritize Safety:** In situations where aggression becomes physically threatening or poses a safety risk, prioritize personal safety above all else. Remove yourself from the situation if necessary and involve appropriate authorities or security personnel to ensure the well-being of everyone involved.

Dealing with aggression and hostility under challenging conversations requires skillful management and a focus on resolution. Leaders can navigate these challenging situations more effectively by staying calm and composed, actively listening, setting clear boundaries, and using assertive communication. Reframing the conversation, taking time-outs when needed, involving mediators, and prioritizing safety are additional strategies that can contribute to a more productive and respectful exchange. With these techniques, leaders can address aggression and hostility with assertiveness, empathy, and a commitment to finding constructive resolutions, ultimately fostering healthier relationships and a more positive organizational culture.

Strategies for Handling Passive-Aggressive Behaviors

Difficult conversations with challenging personalities often involve passive-aggressive behaviors, which can hinder effective communication and resolution. Passive-aggressive behaviors are characterized by indirect expressions of hostility or frustration, often through subtle or non-verbal means. Leaders must develop strategies to address and manage passive-aggressive behaviors, thereby fostering open and constructive dialogue. This section will explore practical strategies for handling passive-aggressive behaviors under challenging conversations, promoting a more productive and respectful exchange.

Recognizing Passive-Aggressive Behaviors

Passive-aggressive behaviors can manifest in various ways, making it essential to recognize and address them effectively. Some common signs of passive-aggressive behaviors include:

1. **Sarcasm or Backhanded Compliments:** Passive-aggressive individuals may use sarcastic remarks or backhanded compliments to convey their frustration or disapproval without directly addressing the issue.

   _____

   _____

2. **Procrastination or Deliberate Inefficiency:** They may intentionally delay or procrastinate tasks or work assignments, creating inconvenience or frustration for others involved.

   _____

   _____

3. **Silent Treatment or Withdrawal:** Passive-aggressive individuals may resort to giving silent treatment or withdrawing

from the conversation, making it challenging to address the underlying concerns or issues.

4. **Indirect Communication:** They may indirectly communicate their dissatisfaction or disagreement by using subtle hints or nonverbal cues instead of expressing themselves openly and directly.

Strategies for Handling Passive-Aggressive Behaviors

1. **Direct Communication:** Encourage open and direct communication. Address the issue, clearly and assertively expressing your concerns and expectations. Promoting direct communication sets a precedent for honest and transparent dialogue.

2. **Active Listening and Empathy:** Listen actively and empathetically to the person who exhibits passive-aggressive behavior. Seek to understand their concerns and underlying motivations. Demonstrating empathy can help diffuse tension and create a more supportive and collaborative environment.

3. **Address Behaviors, Not Personalities:** Focus on addressing the specific behaviors rather than attacking or criticizing the individual. Avoid generalizations or personal attacks. By

addressing the behaviors, you focus the conversation on finding solutions rather than getting caught up in blame.

_____

_____

_____

4. **Set Clear Expectations:** Establish and clearly communicate expectations regarding behavior, timelines, and deliverables. Ensure that all parties involved have a shared understanding of what is expected. Clear expectations help minimize ambiguity and reduce opportunities for passive-aggressive behaviors.

_____

_____

_____

5. **Seek Collaboration:** Encourage a collaborative mindset and involve the passive-aggressive individual in problem-solving. Emphasize the importance of working together towards a mutually beneficial resolution. You can empower them to actively contribute to finding solutions by involving them in the process.

_____

_____

_____

6. **Provide Constructive Feedback:** Offer constructive feedback to address passive-aggressive behaviors directly and effectively. Be specific, non-judgmental, and focus on the impact of their behavior on the situation or the team. Offer suggestions for alternative approaches or behaviors that promote open and respectful communication.

_____

_____

_____

7. **Encourage Openness:** Create a safe, open, and honest communication space. Encourage individuals to express their concerns or frustrations openly and directly without fear of

judgment or retaliation. By fostering an environment that values openness, you discourage passive-aggressive behaviors.

_____

_____

8. **Seek Mediation if Necessary:** If passive-aggressive behaviors persist or escalate, consider a mediator or neutral third party to facilitate the conversation. A mediator can help create a constructive environment for addressing concerns and finding resolutions.

_____

_____

Handling passive-aggressive behaviors in difficult conversations requires skillful management and a focus on resolution. Leaders can effectively address passive-aggressive behaviors by promoting direct communication, active listening, empathy, and setting clear expectations. By focusing on behaviors rather than personalities, seeking collaboration, providing constructive feedback, and fostering an open and supportive environment, leaders can help individuals overcome passive-aggressive tendencies and contribute to more productive and respectful dialogue. By employing these strategies, leaders can transform difficult conversations into opportunities for growth, understanding, and positive organizational change.

Managing Manipulation and Power Plays

Difficult conversations with challenging personalities can sometimes involve manipulation and power plays, which can undermine the effectiveness of communication and hinder the resolution of issues. Leaders must develop strategies to recognize and address manipulative tactics and power dynamics to maintain a fair and constructive dialogue. This section will explore practical strategies for managing manipulation and power plays in difficult conversations, enabling leaders to navigate these challenging situations with integrity and achieve positive outcomes.

Recognizing Manipulation and Power Plays

Manipulation and power plays can take various forms, making it crucial to recognize them in order to respond effectively. Some common signs of manipulation and power plays include:

1. **Gaslighting:** Manipulative individuals may distort the truth or reality, making others doubt their perceptions or experiences. They may deny or dismiss valid concerns, making it challenging to address the issues at hand.

   _____

   _____

2. **Withholding Information or Resources:** Individuals may use their position or authority to withhold necessary information, resources, or support, creating an imbalance of power and hindering the resolution process.

   _____

   _____

3. **Blaming and Shaming:** Manipulative individuals often resort to blaming and shaming tactics to deflect responsibility or control the narrative. They may engage in personal attacks or criticism to undermine others and gain a sense of power.

   _____

   _____

4. **Emotional Manipulation:** Manipulative individuals may exploit emotions and use guilt, fear, or sympathy to manipulate others' actions or decisions. They may play on vulnerabilities or leverage personal relationships to gain an advantage.

   _____

   _____

   _____

Strategies for Managing Manipulation and Power Plays

1. **Maintain Awareness and Objectivity:** Avoid potential manipulation and power dynamics during difficult conversations. Maintain objectivity and a clear focus on the issues at hand. By recognizing manipulation, you can respond more effectively.

2. **Establish Ground Rules:** Set clear ground rules for the conversation that promote fairness, respect, and open dialogue. Establish a safe space where all parties have equal opportunities to express their thoughts and concerns without fear of manipulation or power plays.

3. **Validate and Assert Boundaries:** Clearly assert and enforce personal and professional boundaries. Clearly communicate what is acceptable and what will not be tolerated regarding manipulation and power plays. By maintaining boundaries, you establish expectations for respectful communication.

---

4. **Focus on Facts and Evidence:** When confronted with manipulation, rely on facts, evidence, and objective data to support your arguments or assertions. Refrain from engaging in emotionally charged discussions and instead present concrete information that supports your position.

---

5. **Seek Support or Mediation:** If manipulation and power plays persist or become overwhelming, consider seeking support or involving a neutral third party, such as a mediator or HR representative. These individuals can provide guidance, facilitate the conversation, and ensure a fair and balanced dialogue.

---

6. **Practice Assertive Communication:** Respond to manipulative tactics with assertive, rather than aggressive or passive, communication. Clearly and confidently express your thoughts, concerns, and boundaries without resorting to personal attacks. Maintain a calm and composed demeanor to avoid being drawn into manipulative games.

7. **Document and Communicate:** Record conversations, agreements, and actions to address manipulation and power plays. Communicate clearly and transparently with relevant stakeholders, addressing manipulative behavior in a timely and appropriate manner.

8. **Cultivate a Supportive Environment:** Foster a culture that values transparency, collaboration, and integrity within your organization. Encourage open communication, provide avenues for reporting manipulative behavior, and address power imbalances to create an environment where manipulative tactics are less likely to thrive.

Managing manipulation and power plays under challenging conversations requires vigilance, assertiveness, and a commitment to fairness and integrity. Leaders can mitigate the impact of manipulation and power plays by recognizing manipulative tactics, establishing ground rules, asserting boundaries, and focusing on facts. Seeking support or mediation when needed, practicing assertive communication, documenting interactions, and cultivating a supportive environment contribute to addressing manipulative behaviors effectively. By employing these strategies, leaders can ensure that difficult conversations remain focused on resolution, foster healthy relationships, and promote a culture of trust and respect within the organization.

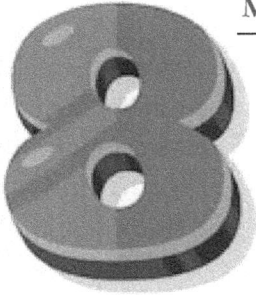

Maintaining Emotional Resilience

Emotional resilience is crucial for leaders in difficult conversations with challenging personalities. These conversations can be emotionally charged and mentally draining, making it essential to develop the ability to stay calm, composed, and focused. This section will examine the significance of self-care and stress management techniques in promoting emotional well-being. We will explore strategies for developing emotional resilience in challenging situations, such as practicing mindfulness, cultivating positive coping mechanisms, and seeking support when needed. By prioritizing our emotional well-being and equipping ourselves with tools to bounce back from adversity, leaders can maintain their effectiveness and navigate difficult conversations with grace and resilience.

Self-Care and Stress Management Techniques

Engaging in difficult conversations with challenging personalities can be emotionally and mentally challenging for leaders. It is essential to prioritize self-care and employ stress management techniques to maintain well-being and effectiveness. Leaders can navigate difficult conversations with resilience, empathy, and clarity by prioritizing self-care, managing stress effectively, and promoting a healthy balance. This section will explore the importance of self-care and stress management techniques in handling difficult conversations and provide strategies to support leaders in maintaining their well-being.

The Importance of Self-Care

Self-care is taking deliberate actions to promote physical, mental, and emotional well-being. Engaging in difficult conversations can be draining, and neglecting self-care can lead to increased stress, burnout, and a decline in effectiveness. By prioritizing self-care, leaders can recharge, enhance their capacity to handle challenging situations, and maintain their overall well-being.

_____

_____

_____

_____

Stress Management Techniques:

1. **Recognize Your Stress Triggers:** Identify the specific factors or situations that trigger stress. Recognizing your stress triggers enables you to manage them more effectively and develop proactive coping strategies.

   _____

   _____

2. **Practice Mindfulness and Relaxation Techniques:** Incorporate mindfulness and relaxation techniques into your daily routine to promote overall well-being. Engage in meditation, deep breathing exercises, or yoga to promote relaxation, reduce stress, and increase mental clarity.

   _____

   _____

3. **Maintain a Healthy Lifestyle:** Adopt a healthy lifestyle that includes regular exercise, a balanced diet, and sufficient sleep. Engaging in physical activity, eating nutritious meals, and

getting enough rest contribute to increased resilience, improved mood, and overall well-being.

_____

_____

_____

4. **Set Boundaries and Prioritize Self-Care:** Establish clear boundaries regarding work-life balance and make self-care activities a priority. Schedule time for relaxation, hobbies, spending time with loved ones, and engaging in activities that bring you joy and fulfillment. Remember that taking care of yourself is essential for maintaining your effectiveness as a leader.

_____

_____

_____

5. **Seek Support:** Reach out to trusted colleagues, friends, or mentors for support and guidance. Sharing your experiences and concerns can provide perspective, validation, and potential solutions to help manage difficult conversations more effectively. Do not hesitate to seek professional support if needed.

_____

_____

_____

6. **Engage in Reflection and Self-Reflection:** Allocate time for reflection and self-reflection to gain insights into your thoughts, emotions, and reactions during difficult conversations. Use this opportunity to identify areas for growth, acknowledge your strengths, and develop effective strategies for managing challenging situations.

_____

_____

7. **Practice Positive Self-Talk:** Be mindful of your inner dialogue and cultivate a positive self-talk mindset. Replace self-critical thoughts with affirming and encouraging statements. A positive mindset can enhance resilience, reduce stress, and improve well-being.

8. **Engage in activities** that bring you joy and provide an outlet for self-expression. Engaging in hobbies, creative pursuits, or leisure activities can help reduce stress, promote relaxation, and increase overall life satisfaction.

Self-care and stress management are essential to effectively handling difficult conversations with challenging personalities. Leaders can navigate challenging interactions with resilience, empathy, and clarity by prioritizing self-care, maintaining a healthy lifestyle, and implementing stress management techniques. By recognizing stress triggers, practicing mindfulness, setting clear boundaries, seeking support when needed, and engaging in joyful activities, leaders can maintain their well-being and effectiveness in their leadership roles. Remember that taking care of yourself is not selfish but a necessary investment in your ability to navigate difficult conversations, support others, and foster a positive and productive work environment.

Developing Emotional Resilience in Challenging Situations

Engaging in difficult conversations with challenging personalities can evoke strong emotions and test the emotional resilience of leaders. Emotional resilience is the ability to adapt and bounce back from challenging situations, maintaining a sense of well-being and effectiveness. By developing emotional resilience, leaders can navigate difficult conversations with composure, empathy, and the ability to find constructive solutions. This section will explore strategies for developing emotional resilience in challenging situations, enabling leaders to handle difficult conversations with greater confidence.

Understanding Emotional Resilience

Emotional resilience is the capacity to withstand and recover from adversity, stress, and difficult emotions. It involves acknowledging and managing one's own emotions effectively, as well as empathetically responding to the emotions of others. Developing emotional resilience enables leaders to remain calm, maintain their perspective, and make informed decisions despite challenging circumstances.

Strategies for Developing Emotional Resilience:

1. Cultivate Self-Awareness: Develop self-awareness by recognizing and understanding your emotions, triggers, and coping mechanisms. Pay attention to your thoughts, feelings, and physical sensations during difficult conversations. This self-awareness provides a foundation for managing emotions effectively.

2. Practice Emotional Regulation: Learn techniques to manage your emotions effectively during challenging conversations. Deep breathing exercises, mindfulness, and visualization can help reduce stress and promote emotional balance. Recognize when emotions are escalating and employ strategies to calm yourself before responding.

_____

_____

_____

3. Foster Empathy and Understanding: Cultivate empathy and seek to understand the perspectives and emotions of others involved in the conversation. Recognize that challenging behaviors may stem from underlying concerns or insecurities.

_____

_____

_____

4. Build a Support System: Develop a support system of trusted colleagues, mentors, or friends who can offer guidance, encouragement, and a different perspective. Please share your experiences and challenges with them and seek their input on navigating difficult conversations.

_____

_____

_____

5. Practice Cognitive Reframing: Employ cognitive reframing techniques to shift your perspective on challenging situations. Identify and challenge negative or unhelpful thoughts and replace them with more positive and realistic ones.

_____

_____

_____

6. Learn from Difficult Experiences: View difficult conversations as opportunities for growth and learning. Reflect on your experiences, considering what worked well and could be improved. Embrace challenges as chances to develop new skills and strategies for handling similar situations in the future.

_____

_____

_____

7. Prioritize Self-Care: Make self-care a priority in your daily routine. Engage in activities that promote relaxation, such as exercise, spending time in nature, or pursuing hobbies. Ensure you have a healthy work-life balance, set boundaries, and allocate time for rest and rejuvenation. Taking care of yourself strengthens your emotional resilience.

_____

_____

_____

8. Seek Continuous Learning: Seek to improve your communication and conflict resolution skills. Attend workshops, read books, or participate in training programs that provide insights and strategies for managing difficult conversations. Continuous learning enhances your ability to handle challenging situations effectively.

_____

_____

_____

Developing emotional resilience is vital for navigating difficult conversations with challenging personalities. Leaders can enhance emotional resilience by cultivating self-awareness, practicing emotional regulation, fostering empathy, and building a support system. Cognitive reframing, learning from difficult experiences, prioritizing self-care, and seeking continuous learning contribute to developing emotional resilience in challenging situations.

Remember that emotional resilience is a skill that can be honed over time with practice and self-reflection. By developing emotional resilience, leaders can approach difficult conversations with confidence, empathy, and the ability to foster constructive outcomes.

Creating an Action Plan

In today's dynamic and diverse professional landscape, the ability to engage in difficult conversations with individuals possessing challenging personalities is a critical skill for effective leadership and interpersonal interactions. This section of the book focuses on developing a comprehensive action plan to equip individuals with the tools, strategies, and mindset necessary to navigate and succeed in such encounters. The action plan is structured into ten key components, each serving as a building block for enhancing one's capacity to handle difficult conversations adeptly.

Beginning with self-reflection and awareness, it encourages individuals to explore their personal communication styles, triggers, and emotional responses in depth. Through this introspection, participants can identify areas for improvement and growth in dealing with challenging personalities, as well as foster self-awareness of their body language, non-verbal cues, and emotional states during such interactions. Subsequently, the plan guides individuals in recognizing and understanding challenging behaviors, such as aggression, passive-aggressiveness, manipulation, or power plays, and developing strategies for addressing these behaviors in real-time. By establishing a framework for assessing the need for difficult conversations and setting clear objectives and desired outcomes, participants gain the ability to approach these interactions with a well-defined purpose and approach.

Emotional intelligence and self-management, coupled with refined communication skills and techniques, further enhance one's capacity to engage constructively in challenging dialogues. Moreover, the action plan underscores the importance of managing non-verbal cues and body language, as well as employing effective conflict resolution and negotiation strategies. Building rapport and establishing common ground are crucial facets that foster collaboration and constructive dialogue. Additionally, the plan emphasizes post-workshop implementation, prompting individuals to develop an individualized action plan with specific steps for applying the acquired skills and techniques.

This section advocates for ongoing learning and growth, encouraging a commitment to continuous development in handling difficult conversations. Following this comprehensive action plan, participants will be equipped with the necessary tools to not only manage difficult conversations but also foster personal growth, achieve goals, and engage in ongoing development in this essential domain of 21st-century strategic leadership.

i. **Self-Reflection and Awareness:**

    a. Reflect on personal communication styles, triggers, and emotional responses in difficult conversations.

    b. Identify areas for improvement and growth in handling challenging personalities.

    c. Increase self-awareness of body language, non-verbal cues, and emotional states during challenging interactions.

ii. **Recognizing and Understanding Difficult Behaviors:**

    a. Deepen understanding of complex behaviors, such as aggression, passive-aggressiveness, manipulation, or power plays.

    b. Develop strategies for recognizing and addressing these behaviors in real-time.

iii. **Assessing the Need for Difficult Conversations:**

    a. Establish a framework for assessing when and why a difficult conversation is necessary.

    b. Consider the potential impact and consequences of unresolved issues.

iv. **Goal Setting and Planning:**

a. Set clear objectives and desired outcomes for difficult conversations to ensure effective communication.

b. Identify specific steps and strategies for achieving these goals.

c. Develop contingency plans for potential challenges or resistance.

d. Emotional Intelligence and Self-Management:

e. Enhance emotional intelligence by practicing active listening, empathy, and self-regulation during difficult conversations.

f. Explore techniques for managing personal triggers and emotions in high-stress situations.

v. **Communication Skills and Techniques:**

a. Refine active listening skills to foster understanding and create a safe space for dialogue.

b. Develop assertive communication techniques to address concerns and express your needs effectively.

c. Practice using appropriate questioning and paraphrasing to clarify understanding and encourage open dialogue.

vi. **Managing Non-Verbal Cues and Body Language:**

a. Increase awareness of personal non-verbal cues and their impact on communication.

b. Develop strategies for interpreting and responding to the non-verbal cues of others.

c. Practice using body language to convey openness, respect, and understanding.

vii. **Strategies for Conflict Resolution and Negotiation:**

a. Acquire practical strategies for resolving conflict and negotiating mutually beneficial solutions.

   b. Develop problem-solving techniques to find mutually agreeable resolutions.

   c. Explore methods for managing defensive behaviors and promoting open collaboration.

viii. **Building Rapport and Establishing Common Ground:**

   a. Cultivate strategies for building rapport with difficult individuals.

   b. Identify common ground and shared goals to foster collaboration and constructive dialogue.

   c. Practice active listening, validation, and empathy to establish trust.

ix. **Post-Workshop Implementation:**

   a. Develop an individual action plan with specific steps for applying the skills and techniques learned in the workshop.

   b. Set achievable timelines and milestones to track progress in implementing new strategies.

   c. Seek feedback and support from colleagues or mentors to refine and improve skills.

x. **Ongoing Learning and Growth:**

   a. Commit to continuous learning and development in handling difficult conversations.

   b. Engage in further reading, workshops, or training programs to deepen knowledge and refine skills.

   c. Regularly review and update the action plan to ensure ongoing improvement and adaptability.

Following this action plan will equip participants with the tools, strategies, and mindset to handle difficult conversations with challenging personalities more effectively. The plan encourages self-reflection, skill development, and ongoing learning to support

    a. Identifying Personal Growth Areas

    b. Setting Goals and Committing to Implementation

    c. Resources and Tools for Ongoing Development

Wrap-up and Conclusion

As we conclude our exploration of navigating difficult conversations with individuals who possess challenging personalities, it is essential to reflect on and distill the key takeaways that will empower you as a leader and communicator. In the preceding chapters, we have delved into the intricacies of mastering these complex interactions. We have learned that effective communication serves as the cornerstone, encompassing active listening, assertive communication, and the skillful expression of needs and boundaries. Additionally, we have explored the importance of emotional resilience, which enables you to maintain composure, manage your emotions effectively, and empathize with others during challenging dialogues.

Recognizing and addressing defensive behaviors has emerged as a pivotal factor in creating a safe and productive conversational environment while building rapport and finding common ground, which lays the foundation for trust, understanding, and collaboration. Furthermore, equipping yourself with conflict resolution and negotiation skills empowers you to navigate these conversations towards mutually beneficial resolutions. Prioritizing self-care and stress management is crucial for sustaining emotional well-being and effectiveness in the face of adversity.

Our journey has also highlighted the significance of non-verbal cues and body language in conveying openness and respect. Ultimately, we have emphasized the commitment to continuous learning and growth as the path to ongoing improvement and adaptability in handling difficult conversations. As we consolidate these key insights, you will gain a comprehensive understanding of the strategies and skills necessary to excel in these challenging scenarios, thereby fostering personal and professional growth in the realm of 21st-century strategic leadership.

Summary of Key Takeaways

a. **Effective communication:** Mastering difficult conversations requires practical communication skills, including active listening, assertive communication, and clear expression of needs and boundaries.

b. **Emotional resilience:** Developing emotional resilience enables leaders to navigate challenging interactions with grace and composure, managing their own emotions and recognizing and empathizing with the emotions of others.

c. **Recognizing defensive behaviors:** Understanding and addressing defensive behaviors in challenging conversations is crucial for creating a safe and productive environment, promoting open dialogue, and finding mutually constructive resolutions.

d. **Building rapport and common ground:** Establishing and finding common ground with challenging personalities helps foster trust, understanding, and collaboration, creating a foundation for more productive conversations.

e. **Conflict resolution and negotiation:** Equipping leaders with conflict resolution and negotiation skills empowers them to navigate difficult conversations towards win-win outcomes, addressing concerns and finding mutually beneficial solutions.

f. **Self-care and stress management:** Prioritizing self-care and employing stress management techniques is crucial for maintaining emotional well-being, resilience, and effectiveness when facing challenging conversations.

g. **Non-verbal cues and body language:** Awareness and management of non-verbal cues and body language are vital in effective communication, as they convey openness, respect, and understanding during difficult conversations.

h. **Continuous learning and growth:** Committing to continuous learning and personal growth in communication and conflict resolution skills ensures ongoing improvement and adaptability in handling difficult conversations.

By embracing these key takeaways, participants will be better equipped to handle difficult conversations with challenging individuals more effectively, fostering stronger connections, achieving resolutions, and promoting a positive work environment.

Final Q&A Session

NOTES

"Difficult conversations are not roadblocks but stepping stones to growth and connection. Embrace the challenge, harness the power of communication, and transform every interaction into an opportunity to unlock the potential within yourself and others."

Dr. Patrick C. Patrong

About the Author

Dr. Patrick C. Patrong is an accomplished organizational strategist, author, and leadership development expert with more than three decades of experience strengthening communication and accountability across the public sector. As President and CEO of Patrong Enterprises, Inc., he has guided thousands of professionals through transformative learning experiences designed to build trust, improve collaboration, and elevate performance.

A former law enforcement officer and national athlete from the Republic of Trinidad and Tobago, Dr. Patrong's leadership journey began long before boardrooms and classrooms. His lived experience—balancing discipline, empathy, and resilience—continues to shape his approach to leading with clarity and compassion.

He currently serves as the Assistant Deputy Director for Human Resources Strategic Initiatives at the Virginia Museum of Fine Arts, where he champions employee engagement, civility, and professional growth. A certified Lean Six Sigma Black Belt, he blends analytical precision with a deep understanding of human behavior to help leaders navigate the complexities of workplace communication.

Dr. Patrong holds a Doctorate in Strategic Leadership, along with degrees in Engineering, City Planning, and Divinity. Through his books, workshops, and keynote presentations, he equips leaders to transform difficult conversations into opportunities for connection, growth, and positive organizational change.

He continues to inspire audiences across the United States and the Caribbean with a single belief: *true leadership begins when communication becomes courageous.*

www.ingramcontent.com/pod-product-compliance
Lightning Source LLC
Chambersburg PA
CBHW070009100426

42741CB00012B/3166